The **Essential** Buyer's Guide

TRIUMPH

TR2 & TR3

All models (including 3A & 3B) 1953 to 1962

Your marque expert:
Alastair Conners

T0386361

VELOCE PUBLISHING
THE PUBLISHER OF FINE AUTOMOTIVE BOOKS

www.veloce.co.uk

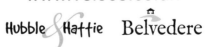

First published in August 2018 by Veloce Publishing Limited, Veloce House, Parkway Farm Business Park, Middle Farm Way, Poundbury, Dorchester DT1 3AR, England. Tel +44 (0)1305 260068 / Fax 01305 250479 / e-mail info@veloce.co.uk / web www.veloce.co.uk or www.velocebooks.com.
ISBN: 978-1-787112-72-8 UPC: 6-36847-01272-4. © 2018 Alastair Conners and Veloce Publishing. All rights reserved.

Introduction
– the purpose of this book

In 1952, the Standard Motor Company, under the leadership of Sir John Black, decided to make use of the Triumph name (owned by Standard since 1945) for a new sports car.

Standard had no real experience of sports car design, and that prototype (subsequently known as TR1), shown at the 1952 Earl's Court Motor Show, was a fundamentally flawed design that would surely have failed commercially, if it had been put into production. However, during the winter of 1952/3, the car was totally redesigned, and from this faltering start the TR2 was born. This was a truly sporting car, suitable for competition as well as enjoyable fast road motoring.

The TR2 was soon entered in prestigious motor sports events by a Works Team and private entrants. In both the Mille Miglia (1954) and Le Mans 24 Hours race (1954 and '55), TRs performed with honour. Many international rally successes followed throughout the 1950s, and for the British club rally driver, a TR was the car to have.

Physically compact, it was agile and manoeuvrable, and – fitted with a rugged and torquey two litre, four-cylinder engine – it had the power and speed to make it a genuinely high-performance vehicle, regardless of cost or size. It was no boulevard cruiser, but a true enthusiast's car.

1956 TR3.

More than 83,000 side screen TRs were produced, and they contributed greatly to British manufacturing prestige. Approximately 90% were exported, principally to the USA and Canada. In the USA, such was the affection for the traditionally styled TR3A that, when the more modern TR4 was released in 1961, pressure from the US market resulted in production being extended for one more year – this model was called the TR3B.

Some 55 years later, all sidescreen TRs are cherished by owners and sought-after by those who appreciate a true sports car, and their dynamic qualities can still be enjoyed on road and track today.

This book is written with the sole aim of giving prospective buyers key knowledge to choose the best example available according to budget. It covers models TR2, TR3, TR3A and the rare TR3B, produced between 1953 and 1962. All aspects of the car are examined in detail, with many illustrations to back up the text. There is also advice on such matters as non-period modifications. Since the 1980s, the TR models have become finite in number, and have increased in value, making it very important to know and understand the points to look for, and the potential pitfalls of choosing a rogue example.

The author would like to thank Ben Freer, Richard McAvoy and Phil Brown for their enthusiasm in providing cars and photographs to illustrate the text.

1959 TR3A.

Contents

The Essential Buyer's Guide™ currency
At the time of publication a BG unit of currency "●" equals approximately
£1.00/US$1.34/Euro 1.14. Please adjust to suit current exchange rates
using Sterling as the base currency.

1 Is it the right car for you?
– marriage guidance

Character

The TR is a traditional British sports car in the 1950s idiom, meaning it has the flavour of a high-powered prewar car, but with increased comfort and ease of driving. It can easily keep up with modern traffic, while making you feel good about your driving skill. The potholes and broken surfaces of British roads (which are ignored by drivers of 4WDs and SUVs) are best avoided, but otherwise these are rugged cars. Rarely, if ever, is a TR2 or TR3 described as pretty (unlike some other two-seaters) but they are undeniably purposeful in both looks and performance.

TR3A ready for the road.

Practical considerations

TRs are of compact dimensions, and will fit in any garage worthy of the name. It is really essential that they are kept garaged (or at least in a secure car-port). They cannot be considered secure in respect of theft, either of the car or its contents, though immobilisers can be fitted to the ignition system.

TR3 ready for rallying.

Insurance on one of the many classic car schemes, with agreed value and other benefits not available on modern car policies, is an advantageous aspect of classic car ownership.

Maintenance costs are extremely favourable – the cars are easy to work on, few special tools are required, and reproduction spare parts are in good supply and reasonably priced.

Interior with 1950s weather equipment.

Prices

Since the 1980s, side screen TRs have been a good investment, but without the meteoric price rises of some other marques and models. At the time of writing, values continue to rise steadily, and there is no reason to believe this will change.

Choices

There is little to choose between the various models as far as driving pleasure is concerned, so your choice will be determined by other factors, such as appearance, condition and specification.

Original style seats.

2 Cost considerations
– affordable, or a money pit?

Parts availability is very good, with most parts reproduced or 're-manufactured,' however, it has to be said that in some cases the quality is not as good as original parts. Generally, mechanical parts are reasonably priced, and thanks to the straightforward nature of the car, labour charges (or your time) to fit them are not excessive. Most bodywork panels and sections are available, but fitting them is a skilled and expensive task.

Parts prices
Prices shown in a range are for different models. TR2 parts tend to be more expensive than those for TR3As.

Bodywork
Front wing .. .. ●700
Rear wing .. .. ●600
Front apron .. .. ●1700-2000
Door skin outer .. .. .. ●100
Floor panel . .. . ●90 (one side)
Inner sill .. .. ●110
Boot (trunk) floor. .. .. ●280

Trim external
Front bumper .. .. .. ●400
Front overrider .. .. .. ●40-60
Rear overrider. .. .. .. ●55
Radiator grille , ,. .. .. ●115-140

Trim interior
Trim kit .. .. ●500
Carpet set .. .. ●190-350

Mechanical
Engine
Piston and liner set . .. . ●400-500
Big end bearing set .. . ●60
Water pump .. .. ●55
Reconditioned radiator . ●310
Transmission
Clutch kit .. .. ●200
Reconditioned gearbox ●500

Brakes
Disc caliper. .. .. ●150-180
Disc .. .. ●20
Rear drum .. .. ●20-35

3 Living with a TR
– will you get along together?

Sidescreen TRs are true sporting cars. However, while in the 1950s they would have been considered relatively comfortable and well-equipped, by today's standards they are rudimentary and without compromise.

Driving

The joy of TR ownership is in the driving. It's possible to drive one as though it were a soft and compliant saloon (sedan) car, but when the driver 'presses on' a little, the car comes alive. The TR rewards skilful and accurate driving, and, more than most cars (even other sports cars), the cornering attitude is affected by throttle input. Throttle response is good and torque is plentiful. The combination of engine characteristics and high-geared steering results in tremendous driver involvement. The chassis has its limitations, especially the rear suspension, but learning the handling characteristics, and honing one's own skill, brings great satisfaction. On the roads for which it was designed, ie winding A and B roads, the TR is capable of surprisingly fast A to B journey times, without the need to break national speed limits. This is a function of a torquey engine in a compact car that makes light work of hills, plus the well-chosen gear ratios, and confidence-inspiring brakes (especially those equipped with disc brakes). Pedal effort on drum brakes is greater than many people are used to, and the down-side of the high-geared steering is that it's very heavy at parking speeds.

All this performance is available with no penalty in fuel consumption. All models are capable of 30 miles per gallon when touring, and a TR2 with overdrive may well achieve 40 miles per gallon. A long range is assured with the generous 12-gallon tank.

TR2 with new seats and fast road preparation.

Cut-away doors lend exhilaration to motoring.

Central fuel filler for large capacity tank.

Hood and sidescreens fitted to doors.

TR3 showing tonneau cover.

Comfort and practicality

The interior is functional and comfortable. Trim quality is good, and the fascia is pleasingly trimmed with clear and well-positioned instruments. For those used to more modern cars, the steering wheel is of a very large diameter, which helps with the effort required at parking speeds. This steering wheel is very often replaced by a smaller diameter substitute. Legroom is ample for tall drivers, but reaching the pedals for those of shorter stature will bring the steering wheel quite close to the chest. There is plenty of luggage space behind the seats and, if the optional rear seat is fitted, a child can sit comfortably. There is a glove box on the dash and stowage in the doors. The boot (trunk) has good capacity for a sports car.

The handbrake is of the fly-off type, and is positioned on the right-hand side of the gearbox cover. This particularly suits left-hand drive models, as it is easily operated by the right arm.

To ensure a weather-tight passenger compartment, the hood, sidescreens and seals need to be carefully fitted. The odd leak can be expected from the bulkhead area if sealant is not used on all joints and mounting plates. Leaks and draughts are very difficult to eliminate. The hard top is not that much better than the hood in this respect, and does increase noise levels inside. For cooler climates and for winter use, a heater is desirable, and demisting the windscreen can be problematic with the original recirculating fan heater. Fortunately, more efficient units are now available.

Visibility at night and in the rain cannot be compared to modern cars. While headlights and heaters can be improved, the rather inefficient windscreen (windshield) wipers are a weakness, though no more than those of any other cars of the same era.

Few now use these cars as everyday vehicles all year round. If wind-up windows and creature comforts closer to a saloon car are wanted, these features are found on models from the 1960s, such as the TR4, MGB and Sunbeam Alpine.

4 Relative values
– which model for you?

By far the most plentiful model is the TR3A, and from the 1960s to the 1980s it was probably the most sought-after. However, once these cars changed from being 'old,' 'used' and 'secondhand' sports cars, and became classic or collectors' cars, this status diminished a little. The TR2, once the dowdy old aunt, became a true original – and increasingly rare. Competition pedigree counts for a lot in some circles, and the TR2 raced at Le Mans and won the RAC Rally. The TR3A did not, though the TR3S lookalike did race at Le Mans.

At the time of writing, values are variable across the range, and depend not on the model, but more on the condition, the specification, and the money spent on restoration work.

Many TR2s have had their cylinder heads and carburettors replaced with those from TR3s, yet this is often not mentioned in advert descriptions. Changes such as the fitting of disc brakes are described as 'upgrades.' These practices are so widespread, they have become the norm.

It's therefore very difficult to say that one model is worth more than another. The price asked and the price paid will depend hugely upon the purchaser's choices and preferences.

The date of manufacture can be relevant if one is considering historic competition races and rallies, where classes may be arranged on a date basis (eg pre-1955 or post-1960).

TR2 showing functional radiator duct.

TR3 with cast alloy grille.

TR3A with pressed aluminium grille.

5 Before you view
– be well informed

To avoid a wasted journey, and the disappointment of finding that the car does not match your expectations, it will help if you're very clear about the questions you want to ask before you pick up the phone. Some of these points might appear basic, but when you're excited about the prospect of buying your dream classic, it's amazing how some of the most obvious things slip the mind. Also, check the current values of the model you're interested in. Classic car magazines can provide a price guide and auction results.

Where is the car?
Is it going to be worth travelling to the next county/state, or even across a border? A locally advertised car, though it may not sound very interesting, can add to your knowledge for very little effort, and It might even be in better condition than expected.

Dealer or private sale
Establish early on if the car is being sold by its owner or by a trader. A private owner should have all the history, so don't be afraid to ask detailed questions. A dealer may have more limited knowledge of a car's history, but should have some documentation. A dealer may offer a warranty/guarantee (ask for a printed copy) and finance.

Cost of collection and delivery
A dealer may well be used to quoting for delivery by car transporter. A private owner may agree to meet you halfway, but only agree to this after you've seen the car at the vendor's address, to validate the documents. Or you could meet halfway and agree the sale, but insist on meeting at the vendor's address for the handover.

View – when and where
It's always preferable to view at the vendor's home or business premises. In the case of a private sale, the car's documentation should tally with the vendor's name and address. Arrange to view only in daylight and avoid a wet day (most cars look better in poor light or when wet).

Reason for sale
Make it one of the first questions. Why is the car being sold and how long has it been with the current owner? How many previous owners?

Left-hand drive to right-hand drive/specials and convertibles
If a steering conversion has been done it can only reduce the value. It may well be that other aspects of the car still reflect the specification of a foreign market.

Condition (body/chassis/interior/mechanicals)
Ask for an honest appraisal of the car's condition. Ask specifically about some of the check items described in chapter 7.

All-original specification
An original equipment car is invariably of higher value than a customised version.

Matching data/legal ownership
Do VIN/chassis, engine numbers and licence plate match the official registration document? Is the owner's name and address recorded in the official registration documents?

For those countries that require an annual test of roadworthiness, does the car have a document showing it complies (an MoT certificate in the UK, which can be verified on 0845 600 5977)?

If a smog/emissions certificate is mandatory, does the car have one?

If required, does the car carry a current road fund license/licence plate tag?

Does the vendor own the car outright? Money might be owed to a finance company or bank. The car could even be stolen. Several organisations will supply the data on ownership, based on the car's licence plate number, for a fee. Such companies can often also tell you whether the car has been 'written-off' by an insurance company. In the UK, these organisations can supply vehicle data:

HPI – 01722 422 422
AA – 0870 600 0836
DVLA – 0870 240 0010
RAC – 0870 533 3660
Other countries will have similar organisations.

Unleaded fuel
If necessary, has the car been modified to run on unleaded fuel?

Insurance
Check with your existing insurer before setting out. Your current policy might not cover you to drive the car.

How you can pay
A cheque/check will take several days to clear, and the seller may prefer to sell to a cash buyer. A banker's draft (a cheque issued by a bank) is as good as cash, but safer, so contact your own bank and become familiar with the formalities that are necessary to obtain one.

Buying at auction?
If the intention is to buy at auction, see chapter 10 for further advice.

Professional vehicle check (mechanical examination)
There are often marque/model specialists who will undertake professional examination of a vehicle on your behalf. Owners' clubs will be able to put you in touch with such specialists.

Other organisations that will carry out a general professional check in the UK are:

AA – 0800 085 3007 (motoring organisation with vehicle inspectors)
ABS – 0800 358 5855 (specialist vehicle inspection company)
RAC – 0870 533 3660 (motoring organisation with vehicle inspectors)
Other countries will have similar organisations.

6 Inspection equipment
– these items will really help

This book
Reading glasses (if you need them for close work)
Magnet (not powerful, a fridge magnet is ideal)
Torch
Probe (a small screwdriver works very well)
Overalls
Mirror on a stick
Digital camera
A friend, preferably a knowledgeable enthusiast

Before you rush out of the door, gather together a few items that will help as you work your way around the car. This book is designed to be your guide at every step, so take it along and use the check boxes to help you assess each area of the car you're interested in. Don't be afraid to let the seller see you using it.

Take your reading glasses if you need them to read documents and make close up inspections.

A magnet will help you check if the car is full of filler, or has fibreglass panels. Use the magnet to sample bodywork areas all around the car, but be careful not to damage the paintwork. Expect to find a little filler here and there, but not whole panels. There's nothing wrong with fibreglass panels, but a purist might want the car to be as original as possible.

A torch with fresh batteries will be useful for peering into the wheelarches and under the car.

A small screwdriver can be used – with care – as a probe, particularly in the wheelarches and on the underside. With this you should be able to check an area of severe corrosion, but be careful – if it's really bad the screwdriver might go right through the metal!

Be prepared to get dirty. Take along a pair of overalls, if you have them. Fixing a mirror at an angle on the end of a stick may seem odd, but you'll probably need it to check the condition of the underside of the car. It will also help you to peer into some of the important crevices. You can also use it, together with the torch, along the underside of the sills, and on the floor.

If you have a digital camera, take it along so that later you can study some areas of the car more closely. Take a picture of any part of the car that causes you concern, and seek a friend's opinion.

Ideally, have a friend or knowledgeable enthusiast accompany you – a second opinion is always valuable.

7 Fifteen minute evaluation
– walk away or stay?

Is the car as described?

Assuming you've made the preliminary enquiries suggested in Chapter 5, and are satisfied with the answers, you may wish to obtain photographs. It's commonplace for private sellers to email photos, and a reputable dealer will do this as a matter of course. Don't make up your mind to buy on the basis of such pictures, as they tend to flatter the car,

TR2 ready for viewing.

and are no substitute for a personal inspection. Make sure that the car on offer has the specification you want. Does the paint colour matter to you? If the car is a colour you couldn't live with then it's best avoided. To achieve a complete respray – that is, all internal surfaces and underside as well as the exterior panels – would require a complete strip down of the car, ideally with the body removed from the chassis. This would be impractical unless a lot of other restoration work was being done simultaneously.

Mechanical changes are more easily made, such as changing from steel to wire wheels, but you should budget accordingly.

If you're open-minded about the specification, and you could consider any of the models, whether an early TR2 or one of the last TR3Bs, you'll widen your choice of available cars dramatically.

If the initial communications with the seller have been satisfactory, and you've decided that this may be the car for you, it's time to visit the seller and inspect the car. Approach this moment with a degree of circumspection. There is a very good chance that the car will disappoint in at least one area, and most sellers will not admit that there are any faults with their prized possession.

Scuttle vent flap from
late TR2 onwards.

First impressions are important. Before inspecting in detail, ask yourself if the car looks as it should. You may find yourself immediately disappointed, and you may not wish to proceed further. Should first impressions be favourable, it's advisable to assess that the model is as described. For example, is it actually a TR2? In the 1960s and '70s, many TR2s were fitted with a TR3A front panel (apron) in steel or glass fibre, either for an updated appearance or to repair accident damage. From the 1980s, TR2s became more valuable than TR3As, and it's not unknown for a TR3A to be fitted with a TR2 nose panel. A more certain way to identify a genuine early TR2 is that it will not have a fresh air vent flap on the scuttle. This feature was introduced at Commission number TS6157, April 1955. Also, early TR2s up to

TS995, March 1954, had windscreen wiper spindle spacing of 10.5in. Subsequent models were at 14.5in. More commonly, later developments are added to the earlier models. Many TR2s and early TR3s are fitted with front disc brakes, but this feature was only introduced in 1956 midway through TR3 production. Disc brakes do improve braking performance, but the price is a loss of originality. The buyer must decide which is more important.

It's almost inevitable that some restoration work will have been carried out, and more likely than not, this will have been extensive. Has this been done sympathetically, to maintain an original appearance? If the car is modified from original specification, are you happy with these changes? Are you looking for a car that requires work, and is priced accordingly? If so, what sort of work are you happy to take on – mechanical, bodywork, paintwork, trimming?

Many TRs for sale in the UK were once export models with lhd, and have been converted to rhd. Has this work been done correctly? (See also Chapter 12, what's it worth?)

Paperwork
Assuming all the foregoing has proved satisfactory and you wish to continue, you can ask to look at the registration documents and check that they're correct for the car in front of you. However, a note of caution, the Commission (VIN/chassis) number and body number are on plates riveted to the bulkhead, and are easily replaceable.

TR3A Commission plate.

TR3A body number plates on bulkhead.

Exterior
Satisfied that the car is worth considering, proceed by taking a closer look at the exterior. Remember that inevitably repairs will have been undertaken, possibly decades previously (unless one has discovered the sought-after 'barn find').

Look at the car from various angles, and check alignment of the body with the chassis. It's quite possible to mount the body on the chassis at a very slight angle. There should be the same distance between tyres and wings from left to right, and from front to back. If misalignment is bad enough it can look as though the chassis and body are travelling in different directions!

Panel gaps on these models were never perfect (beading was used to disguise the gap), but doors, boot (trunk) lid and bonnet (hood) should all open and close freely, without contact with the panels. The wings are all bolt-on, but a certain amount of adjustment was necessary in the factory, even when new, and repair panels fitted in recent times will have required even more hand-fitting.

Paintwork is the easiest of areas on which to pass judgement, but it is worth ascertaining from the seller, if possible, the type of paint used (eg cellulose or two-pack). This will be useful to know, if and when future repairs are made.

Exterior fittings, such as front bumper, rear bumper/overriders and door handles (TR3A onwards), should be present or allowed for, as they are expensive to replace. A tight and well-fitting hood is also desirable.

Interior

A fully trimmed interior is preferable, because the cost of work in this area can be considerable. TRs are not always watertight, and carpets and trim panels suffer from ingress of rain. However, much interior trim and upholstery can survive even sixty years of use, and lend the car an appealing patina. Many cars now have modern replacement seats. These may be practical, but they do detract from originality. The large, wire-spoked steering wheel is also frequently replaced with a more modern wheel, often with a wood-rimmed finish which some owners find attractive, but this can create difficulties with horn and indicator switches (see Chapter 9). Check the floor

Beautifully re-trimmed interior with non-standard steering wheel.

panels under the carpet/matting, especially in the footwells, as rust can be evident here. The same panel on the underside may look fine due to a generous application of underseal.

An overpowering smell of fuel might indicate a leaking fuel tank, or simply that the tank breather pipe is venting into the car. The tank is situated behind a trim panel at the rear of the cockpit, and access for investigation is easiest from the boot (trunk). Leaks from the bottom of the tank will be evident on the floor panels. The breather is on the top of the tank, on the right-hand side, and should have a small-bore pipe leading down through the floor to vent into the atmosphere below.

Rear wing stoneguards showing later model door handle.

Fuel tanks can rust from the bottom.

Under the bonnet (hood)

Look for the correct specification of engine and ancillaries (see Chapter 9 for details). Many examples will have been re-engined, some even with the engine from a TR4A. At a glance, a TR2 should have 1½in H4 carburettors and a 'low-port' cylinder head. An early TR3 should have 1¾in H6 carburettors on a 'low-port' head. Late TR3 and TR3As should have 1¾in H6 carburettors and a 'high-port' head. 1½in H4 carburettors are easily identifiable by their two-stud fixing to the manifold. I I6 carburettors have a four-stud fixing.

Later carburettors and cylinder heads are often fitted to early models for practical reasons, and do provide increased performance, but one must decide whether that's more important than originality.

Make a generalised assessment of the under-bonnet area to ascertain whether this is a well-maintained car. Is it dirty, with fluid leaks, tatty wiring and hastily repaired fuel lines? A gleaming paint job often contrasts with a neglected engine bay, which may indicate a car that is for 'show, not go.' The cooling system is very simple, and excess coolant is expelled via an overflow pipe clipped to the side of the radiator. There is no expansion tank, unless this has been retro-fitted. Remove the radiator filler cap and look for evidence of oil emulsified in the coolant. Be suspicious of a brown oil residue on the underside of the cap and around the neck of the radiator extension – such deposits would indicate a failing cylinder head gasket. Due to the 'wet liner' design of the engine, a failing head gasket can also be associated with leaks at the base of the cylinders, which, in turn, will allow coolant into the oil sump. This is difficult to diagnose without draining the sump, which would be difficult at this stage of a potential purchase. This is why it's important to check that the coolant is clear. Expect to see plain water

TR2 H4 carburettors with two-bolt fixings and correct black painted rocker cover.

TR3A H6 carburettors with four-bolt fixings.

TR3A H6 carburettors with correct chromium-plated rocker cover.

(slightly dirty or rusty but not oily) or an antifreeze mixture in a clean, blue coloured condition.

Many cars have had the cooling fan removed and an electric fan fitted in its place; this is legitimate. If, however, the mechanical fan is *in situ*, and has been supplemented by an electric fan on the front of the radiator, then it's worth asking why that's the case. If the car is used in desert or tropical conditions, the fitment may be justified. If, however, the car is used in a temperate climate, be suspicious that this may be to overcome an overheating problem.

The fuel system is safety critical, and poor workmanship is unacceptable. Check for perished rubber pipes. The early type of banjo fittings that rely on fibre washers for sealing shouldn't be leaking. A small amount of dampness is often found on the underside around the main jet nut; this is usual and acceptable for SU carburettors.

Correct underbonnet appearance.

Wiring is very often in a parlous state, with remnants of old looms (harnesses) cut into, and circuits made with loose wires of inconsistent colour coding. Alternations are often made to incorporate additional loads, such as windscreen washer pumps and cooling fans. An assessment needs to be made as to whether these additions have been installed competently. The original wiring is very simple and includes only two fuses. You may find that extra relays and fuses have been fitted. This can be beneficial but, again, try to judge whether this has been carried out competently. A good guide is how neatly the wiring is installed – is it bound in a loom and clipped neatly to the bodywork?

Underside and running gear

Look for obvious signs of accident damage to the chassis. Parking nose first against high kerbs can cause damage to the front of the main chassis members. Does the car look well-maintained? Are the grease nipples visible or caked in mud or paint? Some oil leakage is to be expected, most obviously at the engine/ gearbox bellhousing joint. If this area has been wiped dry, yet the rest of the underside is dirty and neglected, then suspect a serious leak. This may be from the crankshaft rear seal or the gearbox input shaft front seal. If possible, see if the rear of the gearbox/overdrive unit is leaking and on the axle, check the

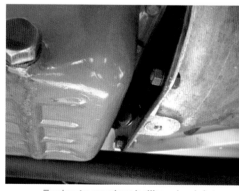

Engine to gearbox bellhousing joint to be checked for oil leaks.

pinion seal at the front of the housing where the propshaft bolts on. The exhaust is a straightforward design and should not have obvious repairs, such as bandage and filler.

Driving

First, it will be necessary to hear the engine running with bonnet open. Some sellers will have the engine warmed up when you arrive. This may be because they've thoughtfully given it a test drive, or it may be to disguise a cold-start problem.

The TR engine is not silent, and some tappet (lifter) noise is to be expected. An alloy valve cover disguises this noise, but there should be no clonks, rattles or rumbles. With the engine running, gently depress the clutch pedal and listen for any noises or change of noise. A squeal usually indicates a worn clutch release bearing. Rattles and grinding noises may be the same bearing, or the gearbox input/primary motion shaft. Worn crankshaft thrust bearings can contribute, and any such noises would need to be considered against the price asked for the car.

If a test drive is possible, then remember that there is no synchromesh on first gear unless a TR4 gearbox is fitted (see Chapter 17). The handbrake is the fly-off type, ie the button is used to apply the brake but not to release it, which is done by pulling up briefly, then letting go. First and second gears are not entirely silent but should not howl. Third and fourth gears are quiet. Drum-braked models may surprise buyers used to disc-braked cars. The pedal can feel dead, but if well-adjusted, the car should pull up evenly without grabbing. Steering is heavy at parking speeds, and does not have strong self-centring, but it is direct, and the car should steer straight and true. With the engine warm, oil pressure at 2000rpm plus should ideally be 70lb/in, but on a well-used engine it may be down to 55lb/in; this need not be the cause of great concern. In normal running, the coolant temperature should be approximately 185 degrees Fahrenheit (85 degrees Centigrade). By now, you should know if this is a car you'd be interested in buying. All the judgements made need to be balanced against the price asked. Double-check the key points (see Chapter 8). If all is well then a full examination should be undertaken (see Chapter 9).

Ready for test drive.

8 Key points

– where to look for problems

Bodywork

Inner sills

These aren't visible without looking underneath the car, and they're crucial to the structural integrity of the body. They mount on four chassis outriggers and support the central portion of the car, and actually join front to back. Rust must be removed.

Wings

Front wings rot from the bottom, so check for substandard repairs. Wing joints to body – while bolt-on wings sound like a good idea for easy removal, rust and rot can be found on both sides of the joint, and the fixing bolts rust into the captive nuts.

Floors

Often rusty, especially in the footwells. Replacements are available, but they'll need hand-fitting. The boot floor can also be rusty, especially underneath the fuel tank.

Chassis outrigger and inner sill mounting point.

Rear inner wing showing captive nuts for bolt-on wings.

A stripped body structure – it is easy to check for rust when in this state!

Check for leaks and rust beneath fuel tank.

Chassis
A true and straight chassis is essential, but it's hard to confirm with a visual inspection. Check that wheel-alignment, front to rear, looks correct. Check that front wheel camber is equal left to right – there should be a small amount of positive camber (unless suspension is modified), ie front wheels lean out towards the top. Unequal camber can have various causes that would need investigation – chassis, wishbones, springs, vertical link and stub axles will need to be checked.

Mechanical
The engine and transmission are straightforward and robust. Problems here are easier to fix than bodywork and chassis troubles. See Chapters 7 and 9.

Trim
Weather equipment: hood and sidescreens should be present and useable.

Ask to see hood and sidescreens erected.

9 Serious evaluation
– 60 minutes for years of enjoyment

This chapter has a number of subsections that can be scored from (4) excellent, down to (1) poor, and there's an evaluation procedure at the end of the chapter.

If you've made the initial assessments detailed in Chapter 7, then it's time to really examine the car in detail, to absolutely know what you'll be spending your money on.

Many sellers will, intentionally or otherwise, distract you with conversation about the car, cars in general or nearly any subject that comes to mind. Try not to be lured into such chat – the seller will rarely tell you about the car's faults!

If you know you'll be removing the body for restoration or replacement, you may consider the rolling chassis and mechanical items more important, but for most purchasers who are hoping to buy a good useable car, the body structure is the best place to start your examination.

Paint mis-match, yet both are Sebring White from reputable paint suppliers.

Paintwork   4 3 2 1

Nearly all cars will have been resprayed by now, and not always in the correct colour. One or more panels may be of a slightly different shade than the rest of the car. This is most likely due to accident damage repairs, or rust and poor paint matching, or paint fading from age. As such, it's not necessarily a cause for concern if it's an 'honest' repair, but try to decide which is the recently repainted area and which is the older and more original. At this point you're looking for body filler disguising rust holes or deep dents. By holding a small magnet in one's hand it's possible to detect a thick layer of filler – the magnetic pull of the steel will be reduced and the magnet may fall off the panel. Repairs of this sort are unacceptable on a car such as the TR, and you should be wary if you find one – corners will have been cut elsewhere.

Many dents can hide behind filler.

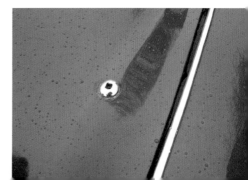

Stainless steel front wing beading.

The bolt-on wings should have clearly defined joints with the main body, and the joint or gap should be filled with beading – body colour plastic on TR2s and half-round stainless steel on TR3s.

Look for overspray on surrounding surfaces. A light dusting of top coat will often be found on suspension components or chassis, indicating careless spray repairs. All engine bays and reverse surfaces of panels should be body colour (except for the prototype and pre-prototype TR2s, which had a

Rear wings fixed without beading make for a less attractive joint.

black-painted engine bay). Expect to find black undersealing on the underside of the car. This unfortunately covers up blemishes. Looking behind trim panels may reveal original paint colours, but not in every case.

The only way to be sure of the correct (original) colour for a TR is to view the factory build records. These are available from the British Motor Industry Heritage Trust (BMIHT) at Gaydon in the UK. The current owner may have purchased such a certificate, and if it confirms the car has the correct paint and trim combination, this can be considered a plus point.

If you're happy with the overall effect of the paintwork on the upper and outer surfaces, then continue by evaluating the integrity of the body structure.

Rear outer wing removed showing inner body pressing.

Removing panels and trim can reveal samples of factory-fresh paint, even on cars that have been painted a different colour.

Outer panels

The wings bolt onto the inner body, which allowed for easy panel removal when the car was in its youth. Today, some sixty years later, the bolts (actually set screws) will have rusted into the captive nuts, and corrosion is likely at the flange joints. Front wings: open the doors and examine the wing joint adjacent to the door hinges. The lower part of the wing attaches to the inner sill, and this area is the most likely to suffer severe corrosion. Water and road dirt can accumulate in a cavity formed by the outer wing, sill and the side of the bulkhead. There should be a steel splashguard with rubber seals at the rear of the wheelarch to prevent road water and mud being thrown back into the cavity, but there will inevitably be a build up of deposits over the years. This is made worse by water running off the bulkhead and draining along the wing joint into the cavity. Repair sections for the lower part of the wings are available. Rear wings: these are simpler and lighter in construction than front wings and there are no rust traps – just check the joints wherever they're visible. Beware of extra thick underseal, which may have been applied to cover corroded metal.

Right-hand side rust trap to rear of front wing, with wing and splash panel removed. This needs careful checking.

Left-hand side rust trap – corrosion here can affect sill, floor and bulkhead.

Bonnet (hood), boot (trunk) and doors   4 3 2 1

Only the door bottoms are prone to rust and they're easy to check. The boot and bonnet are both well-made and braced, and will probably only need checking for obvious blemishes and repairs. If you are viewing a TR2, it may have bonnet release catches with a pull lever inside the car. This is a feature of the earlier models and was subsequently replaced with externally opening Dzus fasteners. Conversely, the boot lid during TR2 and TR3 production was fastened with similar catches that had attractive chromium plated covers. These were replaced on the TR3A with a locking handle in the centre of the panel. The area that repairers/restorers will have most difficulty getting right are the panel gaps, especially those of the doors. The alignment of the door with the rear edge of the front wing, and the curvature that continues into the scuttle, is very important for a good appearance. It is

Floor panels, if hidden by carpet, need checking.

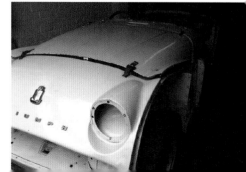

The bolt-on nature of TR panels facilitate repair and restoration work.

also very difficult to correct once welding is completed, so check carefully. The bottom edge of the door should align with the outer sill, but recently produced (and comparatively cheap) replacement sills are simply straight rectangular sections. The doors, however, have a slight curvature, and the result is a door that overlaps the sill. In this case, the

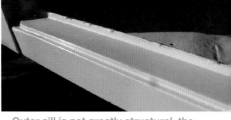

Outer sill is not greatly structural, the integrity of the inner sill is paramount.

welded sill should be removed and replaced with a more expensive item.

Inner body structure

This is where you must make the most detailed examination possible. Any serious rust is likely to be found in the lower parts of the body. You should first check the floor panels, and, in particular, you should lift the footwell, carpets and mats, and check the steel for corrosion. The panels are welded to the inner sills on the outside, and to the propshaft tunnel on the inside edge. The bolt heads of the body/chassis mounts will be evident. The rear of the floor panel, where it meets the inner wing, is also vulnerable to rust. The boot (trunk) floor is prone to rust due to rainwater leaking past the lid seals and condensation running off the fuel tank. The tank sits on a felt strip which, once wet, will hold moisture and cause rusting of both the floor and the tank.

Moving back to the scuttle and bulkhead, from inside the car raise the ventilator flap by pulling the knob on the dashboard, and check both for its operation and for corrosion beneath the flap. With the aid of a torch, look up behind the dashboard to the bulkhead, and check for water leaks and hydraulic fluid leaks from the master cylinders. The former will cause surface rust, the latter will strip paint and destroy carpets. Similar damage can be caused by battery acid spillage plus rainwater trapped in the battery box. Whilst you have your head up the back of the dashboard, check the underside of

4   3   2   1

Floors and footwells can rust.

Footwell, bulkhead and inner wing joints need to be checked thoroughly.

Bonnet Dzus catch on inner wing.

the battery box which is clearly visible in the centre. There may be a drain tube from the box to the gearbox cover – absence of the rubber tube will result in wet carpets and corrosion.

Lift the bonnet (hood) and inspect the bulkhead from this side, and the inner wings. Looking forward and beyond the radiator is difficult, but the most important areas to look at now are the body to chassis mounts. The body attaches at 8 points on each side. Those on the diagonal suspension turret support will be clearly visible at this stage. The foremost mounts are visible by looking under the front apron, and those to the rear are visible from under the rear wheelarch. The body is bolted to the chassis with large rubber washers, packings, and some shims in varying quantities. What one must look for here is stress cracking or corrosion of the attachment points.

Fuel tank sits above axle. Security of the mounting straps is important.

Underside 4 3 2 1

It is now an appropriate time to fully inspect the underside of the car, where these body mounts can be seen more clearly. Also, the quality of any repairs already noted from above can be inspected from the other side.

If the vendor is a private seller at his home, it may be possible to jack up the car and secure it on axle stands (placed under chassis members), remembering all the usual safety considerations of level ground etc. If the car is for sale at a garage or dealer's commercial

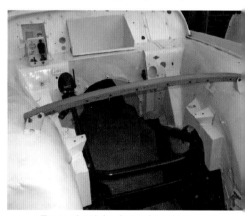

Try to check body to chassis mounts, and look for cracks and rust on the body pressings.

premises, there should be a lift or hoist available. Either way, ensure your safety and do not rush the operation.

Assuming reasonable access to the underside, consider your assessment of the structure by inspecting the body mounting points at the rear by the spare wheel well, the rear floor area inboard, the outriggers to the sills, the front floor inboard, and the front inner wings to the chassis near the radiator mounts. All bolts should be present and rubber strips may be evident between body and chassis, which maintain a small gap and prevent rubbing damage. Check that any weld repairs, such as to floor panels, are finished neatly on the underside – pop riveted patches have no place on a restored TR!

Chasis ④ ③ ② ①

Whilst it's undeniably sturdy, the chassis-wasn't blessed with any rust protection, other than a basic paint covering. Starting at the rear, inspect the two cross-tubes where they attach to the side members, and, in particular, the rear spring hangers where the shackle plates attach. At the front of the leaf spring, the chassis is attached with a large pin which passes through the main chassis member. Inspect carefully for any corrosion here. Moving forward, the central cruciform has a box-like fabrication with the exhaust pipe passing through it. Check this for accident damage – the leading edge can suffer damage from off road adventures. The front of the chassis is the most critical and the most highly stressed area. All the front suspension loads and engine torque are fed into the chassis in a concentrated area around the wishbone pivots and spring turrets. Look carefully for welded repairs, possibly patch repairs on the side members of the chassis, and there may be weld repairs to the lower wishbone pivot brackets. Factory welding was quite neat, so be suspicious of blobs of weld or pieces of welding rod/wire sticking up. These would be evidence of an unprofessional repair job. The very front edge of the main chassis members can suffer accident damage quite often from parking nose first against a high kerb. Damage in any of these areas can cause suspension and steering misalignment, so careful examination will be well rewarded.

Running gear ④ ③ ② ①

While you're looking at the chassis and suspension, check the front brakes – whether drums or discs – for fluid leaks, and look at the flexible brake pipe to make sure it doesn't rub against the front wheel. Careful routing of pipework and the correct length of flexible pipe is critical.

Chassis, floor, outrigger, inner and outer sill structure.

Rear leaf-spring shackle.

Chassis cruciform with exhaust passing through box structure.

Look at the steering swivels and lower trunnions and see if they've recently been greased, or if they look dry and possibly even seized. While looking up, locate the steering box and check for leaks again. Some weepage is to be expected from the gland nut, where the steering column wiring is found. With the front wheels off the ground, turn the steering wheel from lock to lock. This should be smooth with just a hint of tightness at the straight ahead position.

Check the bottom of the radiator for damage and poor repairs, such as filler or solder which may indicate a less than satisfactory radiator. Next, look at the engine sump pan, which will ideally be without dents and scrapes, and evaluate the almost inevitable oil leaks. A slight weep at the front of the engine is to be expected, and a somewhat larger leak at the rear is almost a certainty. It is difficult to know whether oil leaks from the rear crankshaft seal are at an acceptable level or not, and they are easily mistaken for leaks from the front seal of the gearbox, which should leak out through a very small hole at the bottom of the bell housing. The best way to judge the quantity of leaking oil is to check whether it has sprayed back along the gearbox and exhaust pipe, perhaps as far as the central cruciform. If oil leaks onto the exhaust pipe it will burn into a brown sticky coating – if the car has this level of oil deposits you can be sure that the engine sealing is insufficient, and work will be necessary. To the rear of the gearbox there is another oil seal which may cause leaks, and the next component to check is the propshaft. If possible, and with a gear engaged, twist the shaft and listen for loud metallic clicks and excessive free play. Play between the gearbox and the axle can be in the universal joints, or it may be in the crown wheel and pinion of the rear axle. The propshaft has a sliding spline –

Girling front disc brake.

Non-overdrive gearbox mount showing exhaust pipe passing through cruciform.

Handbrake lever and cable beneath right-hand floor.

this should show evidence of being attended to with a grease gun. Moving towards the rear of the car, check the brake pipes for corrosion – these may well have been replaced with copper or copper nickel pipes in recent years, and this material is less prone to corrosion than steel. Also check the condition of the fuel pipe, which will be of a larger diameter than the brake pipes, but may also be copper. Look for leaks at any joints and at any sections of rubber pipe included in the run. Fuel has a very searching effect, and will usually make its presence felt by its strong odour. Take a look at the clutch slave cylinder which should be dry, without leaking hydraulic fluid. It's important that a bracing rod is fitted between the sump pan and slave cylinder bracket. This is often overlooked during restorations and is necessary to prevent undue stress on the bellhousing flange. There should also be a spring between the bracket and the operating arm to ensure a full return of the hydraulic piston. The handbrake cables and linkages will be clearly visible, and should be free moving, with a little slack in them when the handbrake is released. If they appear to be well adjusted and greased, so much the better. At the rear axle, check for excessive leaks from the nose seal, then look at the brake back plates. Hydraulic fluid leaks where the rigid pipes screw into the wheel cylinders are, of course, completely unacceptable. Leaking wheel cylinders may be deduced by traces of brake fluid escaping between the backplate and brake drum. If any residues at this point appear to be not brake fluid but grease or oil, suspect leaking half shaft seals in the axle casing. Check the lever arm dampers for leaks. The only other item to cast one's eye over here is the exhaust pipe, which is of a very simple

Handbrake compensator with cables fixed to rear axle, adjustment of these cables ensures a very effective handbrake.

Check for oil leaks at the differential nosepiece.

Armstrong lever-arm rear damper.

Check damper for hydraulic oil leaks.

and straightforward design, and should pass through the cruciform without touching the box section at all.

These checks are not meant to be to the level of an MoT test (in the UK), but are to evaluate whether the car is generally well-maintained or neglected.

Engine and ancillaries

Reference was made in Chapter 7 to the correct carburettor and cylinder head arrangements. Now it's time to decide whether they are right or wrong, and whether that matters to you. If you're looking at a TR2 and it clearly has a high port cylinder head and H6 or HS6 carburettors, you're looking at a very non-original specification. Such an engine may well be a little more powerful than standard TR2, and the owner may be very proud of these changes and modifications, but you must decide whether you want an original spec TR2 or a car modified to TR4 specification. At this point, check to see if the engine number is still there, stamped on the top face of the cylinder block. Check this against the information in Chapter 17, which may give an indication as to the age of the cylinder block. If a later head has been fitted, ask the seller if the original cylinder head is available to be sold with the car, as TR2 low-port cylinder heads are now difficult to find.

If possible, familiarise yourself with the differences between the various SU carburettors. It's quite common for later HS6 types, as found on TR3s and TR3As, to be fitted as replacements for the original H6s. Without a change of inlet manifold, this results in a shortened inlet tract, because of the longer throat of the H6 casting. A short H6 carburettor will fit on a short TR3/TR4 'log' inlet manifold, but is less than desirable for both gas flow and appearance. Short throat HS6s are best fitted to the long tract TR4A manifold.

4 3 2 1

TR2 H4 carburettors: note the rigid fuel pipe and banjo fittings to float chambers. This labour intensive assembly was replaced on later SU types.

TR3 fitted with later HS6 carburettors on log manifold.

TR3A fitted with H6 long-throat carburettors on log manifold with flexible interconnections to float chambers.

TR2s with H4 carburettors are less likely to suffer replacements, because the larger carburettors will not fit to the low-port cylinder head without a specific, and now quite rare, inlet manifold. Generally, people will have modified TR2s by changing cylinder head, manifold and carburettors (this does require longer head studs into the cylinder block).

All sidescreen TRs were fitted with a very similar type of exhaust manifold, which is a cast iron collector for the four ports, and meets the exhaust pipe at a flange joint clearly visible beneath the inlet manifold. This design (whether high or low-port) did not change, except in some casting details, until the introduction of the TR4A, with a more elaborate four-into-two cast iron manifold.

Anything other than the four-into-one cast manifold will therefore be an aftermarket modification. Should you find that a fabricated tubular steel manifold is fitted, this has advantages and disadvantages. The advantage is a freer flow of exhaust gases at high revs, most evident with modified large bore engines. With a standard specification engine, the performance increase is marginal. The disadvantages are heat transfer to the inlet manifold, which can cause fuel evaporation, and, depending on the design (eg four-into-one system), overheating of the starter motor due to the radiant properties of tubular steel and the confined space.

TR2 H4 carburettors with two-stud fixings; oil filler and breather cap in foreground.

Exhaust manifold, the design of which was common to all TRs up to TR4A.

The cooling system is very simple, and there is little to check apart from obvious leaks or poor repairs. The radiator has an extension neck to allow for coolant expansion, and a simple overflow tube clipped to the side. There is no expansion tank unless it's been retro-fitted. Water pump life is dependent on inhibitors being used in the coolant, and until recent years many cars were run with straight tap water, if there was no risk of frost. Thus, internal corrosion will have been a problem at some point. Rebuild kits for original pumps are no longer available; reproduction pumps are now for sale. They are of a cheaper, and internally different, construction from originals, but they serve a purpose, and are not excessively priced. It may be difficult to tell if the pump you are looking at is original or reproduction. The type of thermostat fitted is critical for the correct cooling of these engines, and the bellows type which is now becoming available again is essential because, as it opens, it progressively closes the bypass hose, and ensures that all coolant goes through the radiator. Unfortunately, it's not possible to know whether this is fitted without opening up the thermostat housing – hardly a realistic proposition. Ask the seller what is fitted!

At this stage, or when you take the car for a test drive, it's a good idea to listen to the engine running. When warm, the engine should tick over smoothly and at well under 1000rpm – this is not a 'cammy,' temperamental racing engine. Some tappet noise will be evident, especially with the standard pressed steel rocker cover. If an aluminium cover is fitted, expect this noise to be subdued. There should be no clonks or rumbles, but some noise may be expected from the timing chain, especially if (as is probably the case) the sound insulation has been removed from the timing chain cover. Otherwise, there's nothing unusual about the TR engine that you need to watch out for.

Ignition and electrics

Turning to the ignition system, all TRs were fitted with Lucas distributors with side-entry caps. This is another area where modifications are commonplace. It may simply be the fitment of a later type of distributor with top-entry push in terminals, or you may find a completely new design of electronic distributor fitted. The original Lucas points distributor, if fitted with correct components, is a reliable and trouble-free system. Replacement electronic distributors are of variable quality, and there's a half-way house option with an electronic conversion of a Lucas distributor. Again, depending on the manufacturer, reliability is variable, and failed electronic components are less easily repaired at the roadside.

All TRs were manufactured with positive earth (ground) wiring. Many will now be converted to negative earth (ground), which allows the fitment of electrical and electronic accessories, which are almost universally designed for negative earth. Either system is satisfactory according to the demands and requirements placed upon it. A common modification is the replacement of the dynamo (generator) with an alternator. This will automatically be part of a negative earth conversion. The advantages of an alternator are increased output at low engine revs and the capacity

Correct Lucas side-entry distributor, note the coil fixed to engine block as standard.

Original Lucas starter motor as fitted to all models up to TS50000, TR3A.

to accommodate extra loads, such as electric cooling fans, additional lighting etc. Under-bonnet (hood) appearance is altered, and alternators, with their narrow belt and pulley conversions, give the engine a more modern look. With an alternator, it's advantageous for a volt meter to be fitted – the ammeter is principally for use with dynamo installations. Make an assessment of the integrity of the wiring – many cars that have had extensive mechanical changes, and have gleaming paintwork and perfect trim, may leave much to be desired in this critical respect.

Girling separate brake and clutch master cylinders, and Lucas voltage regulator, fuse box and starter solenoid. The small aluminium canister being the flasher unit.

Existing looms are often left in place in those awkward to reach areas, such as behind the dashboard, but are then cut and altered to suit various adaptations. There are acceptable and unacceptable methods of connecting and extending cables. Any car for which top money is being asked can be expected to have a new, even bespoke, wiring loom made for it. TRs, up to late TR3A production, had their wiring looms bound in cotton braiding, after which PVC was used. New looms are often produced with cotton braiding and a yellow fleck, which gives an attractive appearance, even if it's not absolutely correct for late TR3As and TR3Bs. In 1959, Lucas snap-connectors (Lucar) were introduced, replacing the simple bared wire and grub screw connection of wiring to accessories such as voltage regulator, brake stop lamp etc. Components with grub screw connections are thus identified as early items, though some of these are now being reproduced with good appearance but variable internal quality. Looking to the front of the engine, see if the original metal fan is fitted on the crankshaft nose extension. If not, look for an electric fan, which could be fitted on either side of the radiator. Wiring to this needs to be correctly installed, ideally via a relay, and it may be thermostatically or manually switched. A car heater may also be fitted, either of the original Smiths recirculating type, with a pull type switch, or a modern heater of completely new design may be fitted, usually behind the dashboard by the battery box. Electric cooling fans place a significant load on the charging system, and if many extra items are fitted, then an alternator conversion might be necessary.

Combined fluid reservoir for Girling hydraulics.

Hydraulics 4 3 2 1

Also, while surveying the engine bay, pay attention to the hydraulic clutch and brake master cylinders. TR2 and TR3s up to TS13046, Sept 1956, were fitted with a Lockheed combined (brake and clutch) cast iron master cylinder with integral fluid reservoir. Subsequent models were fitted with Girling separate master cylinders, cast in aluminium alloy, with a separate fluid reservoir on a

bracket, resembling a small baked bean can with a metal screw cap. This change coincided with the introduction of a revised stronger rear axle, with a Girling braking system. The Lockheed item has been unavailable as new old stock for some time. A substitute from an MGA/MG Midget has been commonly used, being of similar dimension and design. At the time of writing, a reproduction of the original is available, but the piston travels, and therefore suitability cannot be confirmed by the author. The Girling cylinders are more widely available, even though the original Girling company no longer exists, and it's also possible to obtain "Girling style" master cylinders from a variety of manufacturers (prices vary). An advantage with the Girling cylinders is that they're available in different bore sizes, which can be

useful when trying to obtain the correct balance, with the varying sizes of wheel cylinders and brake drums fitted to these cars. It's possible that a car may have a combination of Lockheed and Girling components, particularly if a front disc brake conversion has been fitted. This has certain difficulties due to different pipe fittings and threads, but you may well find a car with a mongrel braking system.

Steering

Finally, while looking into the engine compartment, take note of the steering column. Up until late 1958, this would have been a long single piece, reaching

Split steering column joint.

from steering wheel to steering box. Over an indeterminate period, going into 1959, this was changed to a two-piece column, which is beneficial for maintenance work, as considerably less dismantling is required when working on the steering mechanism. The clamp joining the inner column halves is clearly visible in the engine bay. An adjustable reach option with a different style of steering wheel was available. If the car has been modified with one of the recently available rack and pinion systems, the appearance will be considerably different.

Right-hand drive steering box with stator wiring removed.

The comparatively rare adjustable steering column arrangement.

Transcription

Transcription 4 3 2 1

The desirable option of an overdrive gearbox will be part of your valuation reckoning for the car, and it's essential that you establish whether the correct overdrive and gearbox assembly is fitted, or if a later type has been converted for use with the TR. It's become increasingly common for Triumph six-cylinder saloon gearbox and overdrives to be adapted to the TR. This is more easily and frequently done with TR5s and TR6s, but is not unknown with the four-cylinder models. Similarly, a TR4 gearbox may well have been fitted in order to obtain the benefit of synchromesh on first gear. This gearbox looks similar to the correct, three-synchro box, but is distinguishable by a thicker bellhousing flange, and a slight alteration to the gear housing casting. Such a conversion is usually accompanied by a change in the clutch, from a coil spring to diaphragm type. If the car in question has first gear synchromesh, it should be readily apparent upon test drive. The correct overdrive unit for a sidescreen TR is the

Six-cylinder saloon gearbox with J type overdrive, sometimes retro-fitted to sidescreen TRs.

Dashboard-mounted overdrive switch, correct for A type units.

Laycock 'A' Type. The popular replacement or addition overdrive unit is a 'J' Type, as found on Triumphs from the 1960s and '70s. The two units are quite different in appearance, and while 'A' Type is correct, it's an increasingly rare item. J Types are considerably more plentiful, and arguably a stronger design. The fitting of a 'J' Type and later gearbox does require an alteration to the rear gearbox to chassis mount. (Professionally made conversion kits are available, so beware of poorly made bracketry. Early TR2 overdrives operated on top gear only. All subsequent cars were provided with three-speed overdrives, a total of seven forward speeds.) The dashboard switch was a simple push-pull on the earliest models, which changed to a prominent pear-shaped flick switch for the three-speeders.

The rear axle of TR2s and early TR3s, ie with Lockheed brakes, has earned a reputation for inefficient oil seals and somewhat fragile half-shafts. Both these weaknesses were addressed with the change to what is known as the Girling axle (due to the adoption of Girling brakes), and replacement of the earlier axle with the latter is widely considered beneficial, even at the loss of originality. The crown wheel and pinion ratios did not change – standard was always 3.7 to 1, but an option of 4.1 to 1 became available, though only with overdrive-equipped cars. This was commonly fitted to competition, especially rally cars. The factory would not supply this ratio without overdrive, because of fear of over-revving in top gear. When you test drive the car you should see approximately twenty miles an hour per 1000rpm in top gear (depending upon tyre size). If 3000rpm gives you substantially less than 60 miles per hour, suspect a change to axle ratio.

Lighting

Lighting equipment was all by Lucas, and the headlights were of the British Pre-Focus (BPF) design, except for certain export markets, such as the USA, where sealed beam units were fitted. The tripod design, which was fitted for some years, is attractive, but all original lighting is barely adequate in today's traffic conditions. Newer technology replacements are available and recommended for serious night driving.

Front, side or parking lights contain the flashing indicators using dual filament bulbs. A flat glass type was fitted on TR2s and TR3s, changing to a domed lens on late TR3s and/or TR3As and TR3Bs.

Rear lights on TR2s and TR3s are unusual to today's motorists. There is a single central stop lamp above the numberplate, and the tail lamps incorporated flashing indicators. At the end of TR3 production, perhaps in readiness for the introduction of the TR3A, this, and the rear panel, was revised with separate amber indicator lamps in-board of the tail lamps, which now doubled as brake lights again, with a dual filament bulb in the modern manner. The central lamp was now used for numberplate illumination.

Lighting is controlled by a three-position (offside and head) pull switch in the centre of the dashboard. Dip control is by foot-operated switch. The indicators are switched by a small chromed lever on the steering wheel boss, as part of the horn-push arrangement. The indicator switch stays still while the steering wheel is turned, if the mechanism is working correctly. There's also a self-cancelling mechanism within. Substitution of different steering wheels can compromise this arrangement, and it's not unusual to

TR3A lighting arrangement with combined side-light and flashers set in grille.

Rear lights, as fitted from late TR3 production, with entirely separate rear flashers.

Correctly trimmed TR3A, with black crackle finish centre panel and adjustable steering wheel with indicator switch in central boss.

find alternative switches positioned on the dashboard or steering column. As the wiring for this combined horn and indicator switch is run through a stator tube within the steering column, exiting via the steering box, any modifications to the steering, such as rack and pinion fitment, will necessitate different wiring installation.

Interior, trim, seats

Changes of interior trim and upholstery were of a relatively minor nature throughout the course of production. However, it's worth noting some of the subtle changes that may help you date the car. The instrument layout didn't change, but the central panel containing the small gauges and switches had a vinyl trim matching the rest of the dashboard, until the introduction of the TR3A, at which point it was changed to a black crackle paint finish. All instruments were supplied by Smiths Industries, under the Jaeger brand, except the ammeter which was by Lucas, but with the same face style. All had a domed glass. If you find any flat glass instruments, they would be substitutes from a TR4A. Seats remained of the same design until the TR3A, at which point a new horizontally pleated cover was introduced, with a deeper backrest padding. From the TR3 onwards, the passenger seat tipped forward to allow access to the optional rear seat.

TR3A crackle finish instrument panel.

TR3A Smiths instruments
with domed glass.

The door card/panel has an opening, the shape of which changed slightly over the years. A TR2 should have a leather-covered door pull, and the TR3A should have a PVC-covered wire pull tucked into the opening, which operates the newly-introduced external door handle. Screwed to the inside of the doors are the sidescreen mounts. On all models up to TS28826, February 1958 (TR3A), these were a chromium-plated wedge type which received the steel bars on the sidescreen. Later models have a pressed steel bracket with a Dzus fastening. The sidescreen design changed with TR3 production to a rigid design with sliding Perspex panels. On opening the door, the bottom edge of the trim panel and metal pressing will be either square-cornered, or clearly round-cornered –

Hinged seat fitted only to passenger side
allowing access to optional rear seat.

TR3A fully equipped interior with
sliding window sidescreens.

this helps determine the body's date of manufacture. The rounded doors were introduced at TS60001, during a re-tooling operation at the factory. These models should also have a deeper spare wheel well, but this is not easy to discern without two cars to compare.

Carpeting became simpler (and probably cheaper) during TR3A production, with the over-the-gearbox cover being of a single moulded piece. The boot carpet was replaced by "Hardura" matting.

TR3A door with pocket and pull cord.

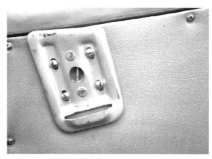

Dzus type sidescreen bracket.

Exterior trim

As befits a purposeful sports car, the TR is not heavily adorned with brightwork. Wing-beading on TR2s was body-colour plastic and stainless steel from the TR3 onwards. A chrome reveal moulding for the air intake could be found on late TR2s, and this continued to the TR3, which then adopted the chunky cellular grille casting. The TR3A grille is an aluminium pressing. Hinges changed from painted to chrome with the TR3.

All models have, on the front apron or nose cowling, an enamelled badge in red and black, with TR2 or TR3 and Triumph lettering. On TR3As, the word Triumph is missing from the badge because, with the revised nose cowling, it was spelt out in bold lettering between the badge and the grille. The badge became blue and white in November 1958. The TR3A also has a one-piece Triumph badge above the rear number plate lamp.

The hood (soft top) is removable and the frame (hoodsticks) folds down

The Dzus type stanchion guide plate for the windscreen allows swift removal of the screen by sliding forward along the scuttle.

Windscreen stanchion fitted to guide plate with Dzus fasteners.

Bonnet Dzus fastener exterior appearance.

neatly below body line. A frame cover was available, and also a cover or bag for safe stowage of the hood. A tonneau was available for open air motoring and weather protection, and when driving alone, the zip arrangement allows for the passenger seat and half the dashboard to be covered. Almost certainly, the hood will now be a replacement, and may be of PVC or vinyl, "Duck" canvas, or Mohair material. If possible, view the car with the hood erected, and confirm that it's a good tight fit. A factory hard top became an option from 1955, usually made in steel (though very early examples were in fibreglass). It's a desirable addition, with the proviso that it's difficult to fit accurately, and it increases noise levels inside the car. Aftermarket hard tops are invariably made of glass fibre.

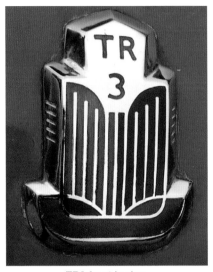
TR3 front badge.

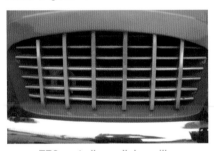
TR3 cast alloy cellular grille.

TR3A rear badge and external boot lid handle.

TR3A hoodsticks in correct beige paint finish. An optional cover was available to neaten appearance.

TR3A hood erected showing rear quarterlights.

Wheels and tyres

The standard fitment was a conventional steel wheel, 15in diameter, perforated with 12 holes, which possibly aided brake cooling. Rim width was 4in, later increased to 4.5in, though the date of this change is unclear.

During most of production, the rim was riveted to the wheel centre, which was satisfactory at a time when it was customary to fit inner tubes to all tyres. Late in the production run, an all welded construction was introduced, and this allows the use of tubeless tyres. Tyre size was 5.50/5.90-15 crossply. Quite early on, Michelin X radials were an option, and late TR3As were increasingly being fitted with 165-15 radials – this would be the usual choice today. Wire wheels were an expensive option, and most cars were supplied with steel wheels. Today things are different – numbers have perhaps even been reversed. Many cars go into a restoration on steel wheels and come out wearing wire wheels. If the car you're viewing is so equipped, familiarise yourself with the types most popularly fitted. The original 4in, 48 spoke wheel is not to be recommended, except for gentle motoring, as it's not strong enough to absorb the stresses of radial tyres, and possibly increased horsepower. 60 spoke, 4.5in rims are the best and most popular fitment, and support a 165mm tyre correctly. Some cars have been fitted with 72 spoke, TR6 wheels of 5.5in width. These are

Steel wheel with original (slightly rusty) chrome hub cap showing enamel globe badge.

Sixty spoke wire wheels with up-to-date vented disc and caliper.

only of benefit if competition is to be contemplated, as they allow the use of wider tyres. However, interference between tyre and wing edge is possible. Steering will be heavier, and stresses transferred to the suspension increased. In recent years, reproduction 'Minilite' alloy wheels have become popular, though they are historically incorrect, being a product of the 1960s.

Test drive

The controls are conventional, though the seating position is different from most modern cars, with legs straight out and the 17in wheel closer to the chest. When the engine is warm, a smooth tickover betrween 600 and 800rpm is to be expected.

The handbrake is of the fly-off type, ie pull up and let go to release, thumb on ratchet button only when wishing to engage it as a parking brake. Do not press the button if you're trying to release the brakes!

When depressing the clutch pedal, there should be no untoward noises – squeal is usually due to a worn release bearing. Original type coil spring clutches have a constant or increasing pressure as the pedal is pressed; if a later diaphragm spring unit is fitted, then you may detect an "over-centre" feel as the friction plate disengages.

On pulling away, expect some noise from the lower gears, but in top the gearbox should be silent. If trouble is found selecting first gear from standstill, do not necessarily fear the worst, it's probably that the car is fitted with the correct non-synchromesh first gear.

On the move, you are hoping to enjoy a car that runs straight and true without pulling to one side or the other. The steering may not be as sharp as a rack and pinion system, but there should be no more than an inch or so free play at the wheel rim. When braking, you can expect drum braked models to feel rather dead on the pedal, and some pressure may be needed to get the shoes to bite. There should be no grabbing or pull to the left or the right. Note that drum brakes are not so effective in reverse. The disc system should give reassuring stopping power.

One of the best features of these cars is the gear change, which should be snappy and positive. As you drive along, listen for clonks and rattles – there should be none. Expect hot engine coolant temperature to be 85 degrees C and 185 degrees F, and this should stay constant, give or take a few degrees, unless an electric fan is fitted in lieu of the crank-driven original, in which case, expect it to occasionally cut in and out. This switching may be evident on the ammeter. Oil pressure would ideally be 70psi above 2000rpm, but 55psi would be satisfactory. Check the function of the indicators and self-cancelling mechanism – it's fiddly and time-consuming to repair.

When you return to your starting place, do not immediately stop the engine, but let it tick over while listening for clonks, tapping noises etc. After letting it tick over for a couple of minutes, rev it up and look for blue smoke from the exhaust, which indicates oil burning. Black smoke would result from an over-rich mixture at idle.

Evaluation procedure
Add up the total points recorded.

Score: 68 = excellent, possibly concours; 51 = good; 34 = average; 17 = poor. Cars scoring over 48 will be completely usable and will require only maintenance and care to preserve condition. Cars scoring between 17 and 35 will require some serious work (at much the same cost regardless of score). Cars scoring between 36 and 47 will require very careful assessment of the necessary repair/restoration costs in order to arrive at a realistic value.

10 Auctions
– sold! Another way to buy your dream

Auction pros & cons

Pros: For the most part, prices will be lower than those of dealers or private sellers, so you might grab a real bargain on the day. Auctioneers will usually have established clear title with the seller. You can usually examine documentation relating to the vehicle at the venue.

Cons: You have to rely on a sketchy catalogue description of condition and history. The opportunity to inspect is limited and you can't drive the car. Auction cars are often a little below par and may require some work. It's easy to overbid. There will usually be a buyer's premium to pay in addition to the auction hammer price.

Which auction?

Auctions by established auctioneers are advertised in car magazines and on the auction houses' websites. A catalogue, or a simple printed list of the lots for auctions, might only be available a day or two ahead, though often lots are listed and pictured on auctioneers' websites much earlier. Contact the auction company to ask if previous auction selling prices are available, as this is useful information (details of past sales are often available on websites).

Catalogue, entry fee and payment details

When you purchase the catalogue of the vehicles in the auction, it often acts as a ticket allowing two people to attend the viewing days and the auction. Catalogue details tend to be comparatively brief, but will include information such as 'one owner from new, low mileage, full service history,' etc. It will also usually show a guide price to give you some idea of what you can expect to pay, and will tell you what is charged as a 'buyer's premium.' The catalogue will also contain details of acceptable forms of payment. At the fall of the hammer, an immediate deposit is usually required, the balance payable within 24 hours. If the plan is to pay by cash, there may be a cash limit. Some auctions will accept payment by debit card. Sometimes credit or charge cards are acceptable, but will often incur an extra charge. A bank draft or bank transfer will have to be arranged in advance with your own bank, as well as with the auction house. No car will be released before **all** payments are cleared. If delays occur in payment transfers then you may have to pay storage costs.

Buyer's premium

A buyer's premium will be added to the hammer price: **don't** forget this in your calculations. There usually won't be a further state or local tax on the purchase price and/or on the buyer's premium.

Viewing

In some instances, it's possible to view on the day, or days before, as well as in the hours prior to the auction. There are auction officials available who are willing to help out by opening engine and luggage compartments to allow you to inspect the interior. While the officials may start the engine for you, a test drive is out of the question. Crawling under and around the car as much as you want is permitted, but you can't ask for it to be jacked up, or attempt to do the job yourself. You can also ask to see any available documentation.

Bidding

Before you take part in the auction, **decide your maximum bid – and stick to it!**

It may take a while for the auctioneer to reach the lot you are interested in, so use that time to observe how other bidders behave. When it's your car's turn, attract the auctioneer's attention and make an early bid. The auctioneer will then look to you for a reaction every time another bid is made. The bids will usually be in fixed increments until the bidding slows, whereupon smaller increments will often be accepted, before the hammer falls. If you want to withdraw from the bidding, make sure the auctioneer understands your intentions – a vigorous shake of the head when he or she looks to you for the next bid should do the trick.

Assuming you're the successful bidder, the auctioneer will note your card or paddle number, and from that moment on you will be responsible for the vehicle.

If the car is unsold, either because it failed to reach the reserve or because there was little interest, it may be possible to negotiate with the owner (via the auctioneers) after the sale is over.

Successful bid

There are two more things to think about: how to get the car home, and insurance. If you can't drive the car, you can hire a trailer (or use your own), or you can have the vehicle shipped, using a local company. The auction house will have details of companies specialising in the transfer of cars.

Insurance for immediate cover can usually be purchased on site, but it may be more cost-effective to make arrangements with your own insurance company in advance, then call to confirm the full details.

eBay & other online auctions?

eBay & other online auctions could land you a car at a bargain price, though you'd be foolhardy to bid without examining the car first (something most vendors encourage). A useful feature of eBay is that the geographic location of the car is shown, so you can narrow your choices to those within a realistic distance. Be prepared to be outbid in the last few moments of the auction. Remember, your bid is binding, and it will be very difficult to get restitution if you get fleeced by a crooked vendor.

Be aware that some cars offered for sale in online auctions are 'ghost' cars. **Don't** part with **any** cash without being sure that the vehicle actually exists, and is as described (pre-bidding inspection is usually possible).

Auctioneers

Barrett-Jackson www.barrett-jackson.com/ **Bonhams** www.bonhams.com/
British Car Auctions BCA) www.bca-europe.com or www.british-car-auctions.co.uk/
Cheffins www.cheffins.co.uk/ **Christies** www.christies.com/
Coys www.coys.co.uk/ **eBay** www.eBay.com/ **H&H** www.classic-auctions.co.uk/
RM www.rmauctions.com/ **Shannons** www.shannons.com.au/
Silver www.silverauctions.com

11 Paperwork
– correct documentation is essential!

The paper trail
Classic, collector and prestige cars usually come with a lot of paperwork, accumulated by a succession of proud owners. This documentation represents the real history of the car, and it can be used to deduce the level of care the car has received, how much it's been used, which specialists have worked on it and the dates of major repairs and restorations. All of this information will be priceless to you, so be very wary of cars with little paperwork to support their claimed history.

Registration documents
All countries/states have some form of registration for private vehicles, whether its the American 'pink slip' system or the British 'log book' system.

It's essential to check that the registration document is genuine, that it relates to the car, and that all the details are correctly recorded, including chassis/VIN and engine numbers (if shown). If you're buying from the previous owner, his or her name and address will be recorded; this won't be the case if you're buying from a dealer.

In the UK, the current (Euro-aligned) registration document is the 'V5C,' which has blue, green and pink sections. The blue section relates to the car specification, green has details of the new owner, and pink is sent to the DVLA in the UK, when the car is sold. A small yellow section deals with selling the car within the motor trade.

In the UK, the DVLA will provide details of earlier keepers of the vehicle, upon payment of a small fee; much can be learned in this way.

If the car has a foreign registration, there may be expensive and time-consuming formalities to complete; do you really want the hassle?

Roadworthiness certificate
Most country/state administrations require that vehicles are regularly tested to prove that they are safe to use on the public highway and do not produce excessive emissions. In the UK, that test (the 'MoT') is carried out at approved testing stations, for a fee. In the USA, most states insist on an emissions test every two years as a minimum, while the police are charged with pulling over unsafe-looking vehicles.

In the UK, the test is required on an annual basis once a vehicle reaches three years old. Of particular relevance for older cars is that the certificate issued includes the mileage reading recorded at the test date, and therefore becomes an independent record of that car's history. Ask the seller if previous certificates are available. Without an MoT, the vehicle should be trailored to its new home, unless you insist that a valid MoT is part of the deal. (This is not such a bad idea, as at least you will know the car was roadworthy on the day it was tested, and you don't need to wait for the old certificate to expire before having the test done.)

Road licence
The administration of every country/state charges some kind of tax for the use of its road system, the actual form of the 'road licence,' and how it's displayed, varying enormously country to country and state to state.

Whatever the form of the 'road licence,' it must relate to the vehicle carrying it, and must be present and valid if the car is to be driven on the public highway legally.

The value of the license will depend on the length of time it will continue to be valid.

In the UK, if a car is untaxed because it has not been used for a period of time, the owner has to inform the licencing authorities, otherwise the vehicle's date-related registration number will be lost and there will be a painful amount of paperwork to get it re-registered. Also in the UK, vehicles built before the end of 1972 are provided with 'tax discs' free of charge, but they must still display a valid disc. Car clubs can often provide formal proof that a particular car qualifies for this valuable concession.

Certificates of authenticity

For many makes of collectible car, you can get a certificate proving the vehicle's age and authenticity (eg engine and chassis numbers, paint colour and trim). These are sometimes called 'Heritage Certificates,' and if the car comes with one of these it's a definite bonus. If you want one, the relevant owners' club is the best starting point.

If the car has been used in European classic car rallies, it may have a FIVA (Federation Internationale des Vehicules Anciens) certificate. The so-called 'FIVA Passport,' or 'FIVA Vehicle Identity Card,' enables organisers and participants to recognise whether or not a particular vehicle is suitable for individual events. If you want to obtain such a certificate go to <www.fbhvc.co.uk> or <www.fiva.org> (there will be similar organisations in other countries too).

Valuation certificate

Hopefully, the vendor will have a recent valuation certificate or letter signed by a recognised expert, stating how much he or she believes the car to be worth (such documents, together with photos, are usually needed to get 'agreed value' insurance). These should act only as confirmation of your own assessment of the car, rather than a guarantee of value, as the expert probably hasn't seen the car in the flesh. The easiest way to find out how to obtain a formal valuation is to contact the owners' club.

Service history

Often, these cars will have been serviced at home by enthusiastic owners for a good number of years. Try to obtain as much service history and other paperwork as you can. Dealer stamps, or specialist garage receipts, score most points in the value stakes, but anything helps, with items like the original bill of sale, handbook, parts invoices and repair bills adding to the story and character of the car. Even a brochure correct to the year of the car's manufacture is useful, and it's something you might have to search hard to find in future years. If the seller claims the car has been restored, then expect receipts and other evidence from a specialist restorer.

If the seller claims to have carried out regular servicing, ask what work was completed when, and seek some evidence of it being carried out. Your assessment of the car's overall condition should tell you whether the seller's claims are genuine.

Restoration photographs

If the seller tells you that the car has been restored, then expect to be shown a series of photographs taken while the restoration was under way. Pictures taken at various stages, and from various angles, should help you gauge the thoroughness of the work. If you buy the car, ask if you can have all the photos, as they form an important part of the vehicle's history. It's surprising how many sellers are happy to part with their car and accept your cash, but want to hang on to their photo! In the latter event, you may be able to persuade the vendor to get a set of copies made.

12 What's it worth?

– let your head rule your heart

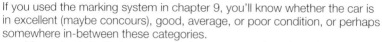

Condition

If you used the marking system in chapter 9, you'll know whether the car is in excellent (maybe concours), good, average, or poor condition, or perhaps somewhere in-between these categories.

Many classic/collector car magazines run a regular price guide. If you haven't bought the latest editions, do so now and compare their suggested values for the model you're thinking of buying. Also, look at the auction prices they're reporting. Values have been fairly stable for some time, but some models will always be more sought-after than others. Trends can change too. The values published in the magazines tend to vary from one magazine to another, as do their scales of condition, so read the guidance notes they provide carefully. Bear in mind that a car that is truly a recent show winner could be worth more than the highest scale published. Assuming that the car you have in mind is not in show/concours condition, then relate the level of condition that you judge the car to be in with the appropriate guide price. How does the figure compare with the asking price? Before you start haggling with the seller, consider what affect any variation from standard specification might have on the car's value.

If you're buying from a dealer, remember there will be a dealer's premium on the price.

Striking a deal

Negotiate on the basis of your condition assessment, mileage, and fault rectification cost. Also take into account the car's specification. Be realistic about the value, but don't be completely intractable – a small compromise on the part of the vendor or buyer will often facilitate a deal at little real cost.

Desirable options/extras

Triumph offered an extensive list of optional extras throughout the life of these models, and if any of these have survived in their original form, they would certainly enhance the value, or at least the desirability, of the car today. A summary of the most common options is listed below:

Wire wheels (48 spoke and 60 spoke from 1959. Often retro-fitted in recent times)
Overdrive (TR2 on fourth gear. TR3 second to fourth gears)
4.1:1 axle ratio (only available with overdrive)
Hard top (for TR3, part of the GT kit. Otherwise available with or without hood)
Heater
Adjustable steering column
Whitewall tyres
Tonneau cover
Rear seat (from TR3)
Windscreen washer
Michelin X tyres
Leather upholstery
Radio

Two-speed windscreen wipers
Fitted suitcase
Tool roll and tools
Anti-roll bar (TR3A)
Competition equipment:
 Competition suspension (stiffer front springs, larger capacity front dampers,
 stiffer rear dampers)
 Aluminium sump
 Skid plate
 Aero screens
 Alfin brake drums (rear on disc-braked cars)
 Dunlop high-speed tyres

Rarely ordered, but available for the TR2, was the High Speed Kit of rear wheel
spats, metal tonneau and metal undertray, as used on the Jabekke Record car. The
rear spats were still available during TR3 production.

Modern options

Too many modifications are now available to list here. They range from modified
components to complete replacement items such as seats. A study of retailers'
catalogues will help with familiarisation, and enable buyers to recognise modern
replacements and additions.

Desirable features to be considered

Originality cannot be substituted, and restoration to the correct specification is not
quite the same thing.
 Provenance is important – full documentation and a long history file can add to
value.
 Factory supplied optional extras, such as a steel hard top, are desirable and
worth having.

The value or otherwise of modifications

It's up to the buyer to decide if modifications detract from or enhance the car, but
you should bear the following guidelines in mind:
 Mechanical modifications that remain out of sight tend to be acceptable. This
also applies to the electrical system, eg alternator and negative earth conversions.
 Substitution of a Triumph six-cylinder Saloon, 4 synchromesh plus overdrive
gearbox is considered a good fitment.
 An increasingly popular non-period alteration is the fitment of rack and pinion
steering, which makes the steering lighter, and possibly more accurate. The racks
are usually from a non-Triumph source, but this isn't considered heretical to most of
the TR fraternity.
 Replacement seats with a bespoke rally style bucket type, or those taken from
a Mazda MX5, are functional but radically change the appearance of the car. Also,
high back and headrests mean a modified tonneau cover is required.
 Conclusion: if buying a car with modifications, be sure you're happy with them –
your ideal may not be the same as that of the current owner, and the modifications
may be irreversible. If the car can be converted back to standard specification, and if
the original parts are available or on offer as part of the sale, then so much the better.

13 Do you really want to restore?

– it'll take longer and cost more than you think

A lot of work is involved in rebuilding an entire body structure.

Inner wing and bulkhead repairs may be necessary.

Repairs completed and front wing trial fitted.

Restoration or project cars are for sale less frequently nowadays. During the 1980s and '90s, American market cars reached the end of their life at a time when there was a classic car boom. During this period, many were saved and restored. Today this supply is drying up, and, as a result, a car suitable for restoration will have a reasonable value as it stands.

The prospective TR owner must therefore decide upon their priorities, as well as their budget. Some of the choices that may be faced are:

a) Buy a car that needs total nut and bolt mechanical and bodywork restoration, and do most of the work yourself.

b) Employ specialists to restore and rebuild the car to your requirements.

If a) is chosen, it may be possible to complete the project at a cost that is less than the market value, and you might make a profit upon resale (although, this is only true if you don't put a price on your own time). If b) is chosen, it's likely to cost more than the car is worth, though this may be the quickest route.

If you're a skilled and experienced mechanic with a well-equipped workshop/garage of sufficient size, option a) is feasible and the end result is very satisfying. This approach also allows someone who can't afford a restored car to become a TR owner, and spread the cost of restoration to suit personal finances.

A middle route is to find a car that needs some work or 'tidying,' but is a runner and not a wreck. Cars of this type are less frequently found today, but are an attractive proposition if the following criteria are satisfied:

The car should be complete, with all original fixtures and fittings, including weather equipment.

It's not structurally rusty, such that body remove from the chassis is required.

Mechanical modifications are not extensive and irreversible.

A TR in this condition can be approached as one would any other secondhand/used car. It should therefore be running, have the applicable test and tax certificates and be capable of road test.

If a restoration is what you fancy, bear in mind that there is a distinction between a 'project' car and a 'basketcase.' The latter is a collection of parts (that may or may not resemble a car) suitable only for major transplants, ie replacement chassis or body structure. Cars such as this used to be broken up for parts, but today their identity (registration documents) have a value in themselves. On the other hand, a good project car is truly restorable, and all major components are capable of overhaul and repair.

Much panel-beating and many hours expended to achieve the correct shape.

Bargain on all four wings needing work

Trial fit of all panels and a sense of satisfaction when everything fits correctly.

14 Paint problems
– bad complexion, including dimples, pimples and bubbles

Paint faults generally occur due to lack of protection/maintenance, or to poor preparation prior to a respray or touch-up. Some of the following conditions may be present in the car you're looking at:

Orange peel

This appears as an uneven paint surface, similar to the appearance of the skin of an orange. The fault is caused by the failure of atomized paint droplets to flow into each other when they hit the surface. It's sometimes possible to rub out the effect with proprietory paint cutting/rubbing compound, or very fine grades of abrasive paper. A respray may be necessary in severe cases. Consult a bodywork repairer/paint shop for advice on the particular car.

Orange peel.

Cracking

Severe cases are likely to have been caused by too heavy an application of paint (or filler beneath the paint). Also, insufficient stirring of the paint before application can lead to the components being improperly mixed, and cracking can result. Incompatibility with the paint already on the panel can have a similar effect. To rectify the problem, it's necessary to rub down to a smooth, sound finish before respraying the problem area.

Crazing

Sometimes the paint takes on a crazed rather than cracked appearance, when the problems mentioned under 'Cracking' are present. This problem

Cracking and crazing.

can also be caused by a reaction between the underlying surface and the paint. Removing the paint and respraying the problem area is usually the only solution.

Blistering

Almost always caused by corrosion of the metal beneath the paint. Usually, perforation will be found in the metal and the damage will be worse than that suggested by the area of blistering. The metal will have to be repaired before repainting.

Blistering.

Micro blistering

Usually the result of an economy respray, where inadequate heating has allowed moisture to settle on the car before spraying. Consult a paint specialist, but usually damaged paint will have to be removed before partial or full respraying. Can also be caused by car covers that don't 'breathe.'

Micro blistering.

Fading

Some colours, especially reds, are prone to fading if subjected to strong sunlight for long periods, without the benefit of polish protection. Sometimes proprietary paint restorers, and/or paint cutting/rubbing compounds, will retrieve the situation. Often a respray is the only real solution.

Peeling

Often a problem with metallic paintwork, when the sealing laquer becomes damaged and begins to peel off. Poorly applied paint may also peel. The remedy is to strip and start again!

Dimples

Dimples in the paintwork are caused by the residue of polish (particularly silicone types) not being removed properly before respraying. Paint removal and repainting is the only solution.

Dents

Small dents are usually easily cured by the 'Dentmaster,' or equivalent process, that suckt or pushed out the dent (as long as the paint surface is still intact). Companies offering dent removal services usually come to your home – consult your telephone directory.

15 Problems due to lack of use
– just like their owners, TR2s & TR3s need exercise!

Cars, like humans, are at their most efficient if they exercise regularly. A run of at least ten miles, once a week, is recommended for classics.

Engine
The main cause for concern with TR four-cylinder engines is failure of the figure of eight seals at the base of the cylinder liners. Lack of anti-freeze/inhibitor increases the chance of this occurring, and this allows coolant to seep into the sump, adulterating the oil. Stale fuel left for any length of time will, in addition to preventing the engine starting, cause corrosion and deposits to be formed in carburettors, metal pipes, and the fuel tank. Don't attempt to start the engine until the oil has been drained, checked for water, and replenished with new oil.

Seized components
Pistons in calipers, slave and master cylinders can seize.

The clutch may seize if the plate becomes stuck to the flywheel because of corrosion.

Handbrakes (parking brakes) can seize if the cables and linkages rust.

Pistons can seize in the bores due to corrosion.

Fluids
Old, acidic oil can corrode bearings.

Uninhibited coolant can corrode internal waterways. Lack of antifreeze can cause core plugs to be pushed out, even cracks in the block or head. Silt settling and solidifying can cause overheating.

Brake fluid absorbs water from the atmosphere and should be renewed every two years. Old fluid with a high water content can cause corrosion. It can also cause pistons/calipers to seize (freeze), and brakes to fail when the water turns to vapour near hot braking components.

Tyre problems
Tyres that have had the weight of the car on them in a single position for some time will develop flat spots, resulting in some (usually temporary) vibration. The tyre walls may have cracks or (blister-type) bulges, meaning new tyres are needed.

Shock absorbers (dampers)
With lack of use, the dampers will lose their elasticity or even seize. Creaking, groaning and stiff suspension are signs of this problem.

Rubber and plastic
Radiator hoses may have perished and split, possibly resulting in the loss of all coolant. Window and door seals can harden and leak. Gaiters/boots can crack. Wiper blades will harden. Rubber fuel pipes will have perished and been eaten away by stale fuel.

Electrics

The battery will be of little use if it hasn't been charged for many months.

Earthing/grounding problems are common when the connections have corroded. Old bullet and spade type electrical connectors commonly rust/corrode, and will need disconnecting, cleaning and protection (eg *Vaseline*).

Sparkplug electrodes will often have corroded in an unused engine.

Wiring insulation can harden and fail.

Damp and surface corrosion will also affect electrical and ignition components. Contact breaker points will have increased electrical resistance that may prevent the engine starting.

Rotting exhaust system

Exhaust gas contains a high water content, so exhaust systems corrode very quickly from the inside when the car is not used.

Interior

If the car has been stored under cover with windows closed for a long time, the interior may suffer from mildew and damp caused by condensation.

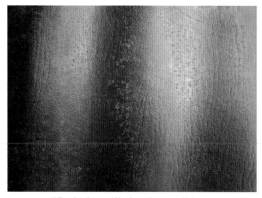

Vinyl trim suffering from mildew.

16 The Community
– key people, organisations and companies in the TR2 & TR3 world

Triumphs are well catered for with both single and all model clubs. Probably the greatest following outside the UK is in the USA, which was the original destination for so many of these cars when new. These clubs usually have social activities, and increasingly they provide useful internet forums, where technical help and advice abounds. The larger clubs have international contacts.

UK
Club Triumph (all models): club.triumph.org.uk
TR Register: tr-register.co.uk
TR Drivers Club: trdrivers.com

USA
vintagetriumphregister.org
triumphregister.com
triumphexp.com

Europe
triumph.nl
trclub.nl
triumph-ig.de
swisstrclub.ch
triumph-club-de-france.fr
trregisterfrance.fr
trregister.be
britisholdtimersbelgianclub.be
triumphtr.com
triumphclub.se
tr-club.dk
tr-register.dk
trclub-spain.com
triumphclub.pt

Enjoying the fruits of your labour on a race track.

The sidescreen cars are also eligible for many competitive activities, and are often seen on historic rally events, where they can be found taking on a varied selection of often exotic cars.
hrcr.co.uk

Authenticity verification
TR sports car owners are lucky in that most of the factory build records have survived, and are held in purpose built archives at The British Motor Industry Heritage Trust: britishmotormuseum.co.uk

Recommended reading

There has been good coverage of Triumph cars in books to suit all tastes. Two notable Triumph historians are Graham Robson, who is well-versed in company history and rallying activities, and Bill Piggott, whose years of research have yielded exhaustive knowledge of TRs. Unfortunately, many of the standard works are now out of print, but they can usually be found second-hand. Some useful titles are:

The Story of Triumph Sports Cars, Graham Robson, ISBN 0900549238
The Triumph TRs, Graham Robson, ISBN 0900549637
Triumph TR2, 3 & 3A In Detail, Bill Piggott, ISBN 9780954998158
Triumph TR2 & TR3 1952 1960, by Brooklands Books, ISBN 0906589568
Triumph Cars in America, Michael Cook, ISBN 0760301654

It's very useful to obtain the factory workshop manual and handbook, and the standard issue instruction book entitled *Triumph Sports Car TR2 or TR3*, various editions. These two publications will tell you all that is necessary to run and maintain your TR.

Parts suppliers

Parts for Triumph sports cars are readily available, which is surprising considering how long the cars have been out of production. Specialist parts suppliers, garages and workshops can be found in most countries that have a sizeable demand. For recommended workshops, consider seeking advice from existing owners to gain from their experiences. The biggest international parts supplier is the Moss Group:

moss-europe.co.uk
moss-europe.fr
mossmotors.com

17 Vital statistics
– essential data at your fingertips

Triumph continued the Standard Motor Company tradition of issuing all cars with a Commission number (they were never referred to as chassis numbers, and all TRs have the prefix TS). Numbering starts at TS1 and continues to TS82346 for the last TR3A. TR3Bs have the prefix of either TSF or TCF. Commission numbers with the suffix L denote left-hand drive. Engine numbers have the suffix E, and run close to, but not the same as, Commission numbers. Factory reconditioned engines have the original number obliterated and a brass plaque affixed with the prefix FR.

Major change points and Commission numbers

TR2		
TS1 to TS8636	July 1953 to October 1955	Total production 8636, some numbers possibly not used (TS1 and 2 were pre-production models)
TR3		
TS8637 to TS22013	October 1955 to September 1957	Total production 13,377
From TS13053E	Aug 1956	High port cylinder head fitted
From TS13046	Sept 1956	Disc brakes and new rear axle fitted
TR3A		
TS22014 to TS82346	September 1957 to 1962	Total production 58,309
There is a gap in issued numbers from TS47956 to TS50000		
408 produced in 1961 and only 7 in 1962		
TR3B		
TSF1 to TSF530	March 1962 to April 1962	Total production 530
Mechanically as TR3A		
TCF1 to TCF2804	May 1962 to Oct 1962	Total production 3334
TR4 engine and all synchromesh gearbox		

The above production figures have been drawn from those compiled by noted Triumph historians Bill Piggott and Graham Robson. More detail can be found in their definitive marque histories, referred to in Chapter 16.

Essential specifications

Engine	4 cylinder in line, wet-liner, pushrod OHV		
	Bore 83mm, 3.268in	TR3A from 1959, 86mm 3.386in option	
	Stroke 92mm, 3.622in		
	Capacity	1991cc, 121.5cu in	2138cc 130.5cu in with 86mm bore
	Compression ratio 8.5, 90.1 with 86mm bore		
	BHP	90 at 4800rpm	TR2
		95	TR3 Low Port
		100 at 5000rpm	TR3/TR3A High Port
		105 at 4750rpm	TR3A/TR3B with 86mm bore

Road speed at 1000rpm. Approximate assuming 165-15 tyres, 3.7:1 Axle							
	24 mph	20mph	18mph	15mph	12mph	10mph	6mph

Steering	2 1/3 turns lock to lock.	
Suspension	Coil and Wishbone front. Semi-elliptic rear.	
Dimensions	Length	12ft 7in (384cm)
	Width	4ft 7.5in (141cm)
	Height to top screen	3ft 10in (117cm)
	Wheelbase	7ft 4in (224cm)
	Track	Front: 3ft 9in (114cm) Rear: 3ft 9.5in (116cm)
Weight	Complete – fuel tank full	2135lb (970kg)
	Dry	2009lb (910kg)

Performance

Straight line performance of all models was similar because power was increased from TR2 to TR3, as weight increased. A 2138cc TR3A/TR3B would be the fastest, but the author is not aware of any contemporary, authoritative road tests. The TR2 was, without doubt, the most economical. The following figures are the approximate average of British and American Magazine road tests:

Top speed 107mph, SS ¼ mile, 18.5 seconds
0-50mph 8.2 seconds. 0-60 mph, 11.9 seconds.
40-60mph 3rd gear, 6.5 seconds. 60-80mph 4th gear, 11.3 seconds
50-70mph 3rd gear, 6.5 seconds.
Fuel consumption overall, TR2, 34mpg, TR3/TR3A/TR3B 30mpg.

Exterior colours

	TR2 up to April 1954	TR2 up to Sep 1955	TR3	TR3A	TR3B
Geranium	•				
Ice Blue	•				
Olive Yellow	•	•	•	•	
Pearl White	•	•	•	Becomes Sebring White then Spa White	•
Black	•	•	•	•	•
British Racing Green		•	•	•	
Signal Red		•	•	•	•
Salvador Blue then Winchester Blue			•	•	
Beige			•	•	
Apple Green/ Avocado Green			•	•	
Pearl Grey, later Silverstone Grey				•	
Powder Blue				•	•
Primrose Yellow, later Pale Yellow				•	

Interior trim colours were generally as exterior paint in certain prescribed combinations, though there were some trim colours not available as paint.

TR2: Grey, Blackberry, Stone, Brown.
TR3: Vermillion
TR3A: Targo Purple
TR3B: Midnight Blue

It's believed that colours of personal choice were available as a special order, and some cars are known to have been finished in metallic paint.

Also from Veloce:

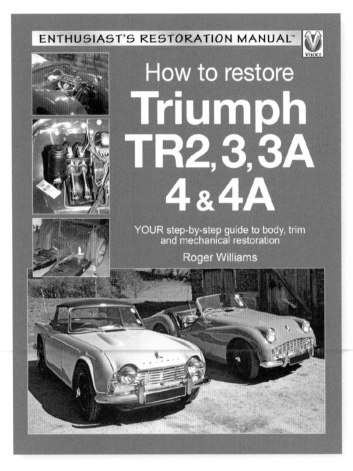

ISBN: 978-1-845849-47-4
Paperback • 27x20.7cm • 208 pages • 500 pictures

Available again after a long absence!
This book, which covers all Triumph TR2, 3, 3A, 4 & 4A models, explains the
characteristics of the different models, what to look out for when purchasing
and how to restore a TR cost effectively.

Veloce *Classic Reprint* Series

GREAT CARS

TRIUMPH
TR

TR2 to 6: The last of the traditional sports cars

BILL PIGGOTT

ISBN: 978-1-845848-54-5
Hardback • 25x25cm • 160 pages • 295 pictures

The Triumph TR range has earned its place among the most popular sports cars of all time, with enthusiasts and owners on both sides of the Atlantic. The cars covered here range from the original, basic, four-cylinder TR2 of 1953, to the hairy-chested six-cylinder TR6 that finally bowed out of production in 1975, replaced by the TR7.

The Essential Buyer's Guide™ series ...

... don't buy a vehicle until you've read one of these!

Index